THE ROAD GOES
EVER ON

BOOKS BY

J. R. R. Tolkien

THE HOBBIT

FARMER GILES OF HAM

THE LORD OF THE RINGS
The Fellowship of the Ring
The Two Towers
The Return of the King

THE ADVENTURES OF TOM BOMBADIL

TREE AND LEAF

THE ROAD GOES EVER ON

SIR GAWAIN AND THE GREEN KNIGHT

THE FATHER CHRISTMAS LETTERS

THE SILMARILLION

THE ROAD GOES EVER ON

A SONG CYCLE

POEMS BY J. R. R. TOLKIEN

MUSIC BY DONALD SWANN

with decorations by J. R. R. Tolkien

SECOND EDITION, REVISED

HOUGHTON MIFFLIN COMPANY BOSTON

1978

Library of Congress Catalog Card Number 67–20501
ISBN: 0–395–24758–6

Printed in the United States of America

H   10   9   8   7   6   5   4   3   2   1

FOREWORD

to the Second Edition

For the publication of the song cycle *The Road Goes Ever On* in 1967, I wrote a foreword explaining how I had fallen under the spell of Tolkien's *Lord of the Rings,* and how certain poems had grouped themselves in my imagination — about the Road. I have more to add to this foreword now, but I will first retell the origin of the songs, born of my travels over ten years back.

After my wife had communicated to me her passion for the three volumes of *The Lord of the Rings,* we found we were reading them more or less every spring. This raised a special problem when we were about to go to Australia by air and the hard covers weighed too much to carry. (At that time British readers marched under hard covers exclusively.) I was setting out on a tour of *At the Drop of a Hat* in August 1964 and returning in March 1965. The Australian spring begins in October and we did not want to be without the books. After much deliberation we put the volumes, along with other items, into a steel trunk and sent them off a few months

ahead. At the end of the tour the trunk was being packed up for the return sea journey while the Swann family was taking another route via Japan, Iran and Jordan. My wife suggested that I copy out some lyrics from the three books and set them to music en route. I had been performing for four months and I had an appetite for composing. That is how the first six songs came to be written on a beautiful Steinway grand piano in Ramallah outside Jerusalem. The hills outside Jerusalem are extremely lovely, and if the caves around the Dead Sea are the place for old scrolls, they could as well be the place for hobbits: many of the caves are round, dry and extensive.

On my return to England the firm of George Allen and Unwin was good enough to give me permission to use the lyrics, and also to put me in touch with Professor Tolkien. At a delightful tea party in Oxford at the home of his daughter, Priscilla, the Professor approved five but hesitated over my music for "Namárië," Galadriel's farewell in Lorien. He had heard it differently in

his mind, he said, and hummed a Gregorian chant. I made a note of it, and in the following week I played it over many times to the Elvish words. There was no doubt that this monodic line from an early Church music tradition expressed the words ideally, not only the sadness of the word "Namárië," and the interjection "Ai!," but equally the ritual mood of the Elves. For my song cycle it would make a variation for the piano to stop, and then return for the next song. So I added only the introductory line, interlude and coda. Number five is thus words and theme by Professor Tolkien.

In Sydney, when I was selecting lyrics from *The Lord of the Rings*, I searched for the short evocative poems of mood and atmosphere. As I came to them, I was struck by their clarity and concision, and I began to feel their flavour as poems outside the narrative in which they appear. The longer ballads seemed self-sufficient. Rugged, rumbustious and rollicking, they swept on like huge rivers. Not for me to plunge into them. But the shorter ones looked as if they would enjoy musical accompaniment, and every creature in them was on the road — Bilbo, who sets the pace, Frodo and Sam journeying to the Mountains of Doom, Treebeard herding his trees — everyone was moving. So I called the cycle *The Road Goes Ever On*, and this is also the title of the first song. Its tune is echoed in the sixth, and again in "Errantry," which I added later, composing it on yet another tour in the USA. This is a huge poem, but as soon as I saw it, in *The Adventures of Tom Bombadil*, I felt it was pure music. These songs of Middle-Earth were thus composed in the Middle East and the Middle West!

Eight, nearly nine years have passed, and I have lost two good friends, Professor Ronald and Mrs. Edith Tolkien. I have also lost my friend Michael Flanders. The landscape on the Road now seems different, and yet the song cycle still speaks to me, and has even grown. Soon after the Professor's death, Joy Hill, who had for many years acted as Tolkien's secretary on behalf of his publishers, handed me "Bilbo's Last Song." The poem was a farewell gift to her from the Professor and she was very moved by it. I understand the poem was written a good many years ago, and its appearance in the last year of Tolkien's life was but more evidence of the wealth of unpublished material, now being examined and edited by his son Christopher. The poem moved me, too, and I set it to music. As I did this, a host of impressions came back to me, chapters in my association with the world of Tolkien. There is no particular order unless it be vaguely chronological, so I will give them headings, like this:

OBSERVATION I. I had but to write down one song and play it to the first hearer, to find that each person feels about *The Lord of the Rings* in his own way. I discovered that at the moment when you set music to a poem you are quite alone, even though your lyric writer's work is well-loved by a large public. Yet my meetings with the Professor and with his wife, who had played the piano to concert standard, heartened me immensely, for I suddenly felt that the piano,

instead of being the last instrument you would expect to see in Middle-Earth, had some close connection with Tolkien's imagination. This was a great relief.

EPISODE I. The publication of the song book, and the subsequent recording by the bass-baritone William Elvin (now of Covent Garden Opera House) was an invigorating experience. It was marvellous to see Tolkien's beautiful Elvish script shown in all its elegance. He unexpectedly contributed a glossary which contained information about the Elvish language, and indeed about the Elves, that had not appeared anywhere else. I discovered then that Tolkien's calligraphy, his scholarship and his inventiveness were all one thing.

EPISODE II. Singing a Tolkien setting in *At the Drop of a Hat* effected a link between Michael Flanders and Tolkien. The Professor had a vast admiration for Michael Flanders' lyrics. They both adored words and the adept use of them. They met backstage after one of our performances at the New Theatre, Oxford. This reminded me of the vein of Oxford University fantasy (Michael had been, like me, at Christ Church). Michael's courting armadillos on Salisbury Plain are, to my mind, cousins to the flamingos in Lewis Carroll's *Alice;* to the Hrossa of C. S. Lewis; and the talking eagles of Tolkien.

OBSERVATION II. I encountered the Tolkien cult in the USA in 1966, and soon felt its kinship to certain American sub-cultures; indeed, the Tolkien cult seemed to reflect the strong American urge for varying life styles, such as the Pennsylvania Amish, compulsively rural, like the Shire hobbits.

1966 still had its flower children in hippy garb. " 'Supper is ready,' said Goldberry; and now the hobbits saw that she was clothed all in silver with a white girdle, and her shoes were like fishes' mail. But Tom was all in clean blue, blue as rain-washed forget-me-nots, and he had green stockings." Is there a kinship even here?

Some remarkably naïve thinking and bad art has been pinned onto the name of Tolkien, but the "cultists" I met then in America were undoubtedly book lovers. If a few expressed their devotion by sending parcels of mushrooms to the Professor, this was but an expression of constant reading and re-reading of *The Lord of the Rings.* I know the cult puzzled and sometimes annoyed the Professor, and that some of the fans became a nuisance to him. But living for some time in the States, I have become accustomed to enthusiasts of all kinds. I think I may even have helped think up the lapel button "Gandalf for President." I often wish he were.

OBSERVATION III. Back in England, playing the Song Cycle in concerts, I noted that about a quarter of a general audience knew *The Lord of the Rings* and were especially interested in the words that were being sung. For the remaining three-quarters I had to be careful about how much I said before the music began. If I told them "I Sit Beside the Fire" was a meditation by a 130-year-old hobbit, it only produced a confused impression in their minds when they heard the quiet elegiac lines. If I told them the next song would be in Elvish, they wondered if it were some kind of children's game I was playing; and to explain "In the Willow-meads of Tasarinan" as a song by a walking tree seemed impossible. I am indebted to Roger Cleverdon, a bass who sings Treebeard's song beautifully, for this useful introductory line: "Think of one of those road-signs: CAUTION HEAVY PLANT CROSSING."

OBSERVATION IV. My interest in religious ideas and music brought me into touch with numerous people for whom Tolkien's books were a kind of Christian beacon. I read Tolkien's essay "Tree and Leaf," where he explores fascinatingly the matter of happy endings in faery stories and the way in which happy endings pattern the Resurrection. I began to see a connection between Tolkien's Catholic beliefs (including the Gregorian tune he had hummed to me) and the feudal but noble world in which his Middle-Earth creatures lived.

EPISODE III. I took a holiday near Limerick in Eire, and suddenly lived where there are very few cars and no industry. This set me thinking of the ubiquitous *green* in *The Lord of the Rings* (the publishers, under this spell, have produced our new edition with green as the second colour!). Tolkien now shone forth to me as the forerunner of the conservationists, the man who stood for forests and fields over against slag heaps and concrete jungles. Having chosen myself to live in Battersea in South London, best known for its

power station, I wondered whether his instinct had carried him too far. But there is surely no doubt that he foresaw the era in which we now live, when the "age of technology" is about to be balanced by a more Franciscan attitude, and the extinction of an animal species now hurts young people as much as, earlier, the introduction of a new brand of motorbike pleased them.

OBSERVATION V. Along with many others I often found myself desiring to vanish into Middle-Earth, to escape utterly into fantasy! On the one hand this was a temptation making one unfit to live in this earth at all; on the other, the phrase Middle-Earth is but a mediaeval way of describing our own world poised between Heaven and Hell. Is Tolkien's world of fantasy an escape at all, or do we therein meet ourselves, with all our problems? His books, as those of C. S. Lewis, include well-nigh perfect creatures, Elves, eldila, great lords and magicians. These heroes, I decided, were but paradigms of humans with a sense of destiny and purpose; and Frodo, the central hero, carries mortality in the shape of a lasting wound. The heroes of Greek legend were often real people of a past time, only with wings drawn in. To sum up this paragraph, I used to feel that the Tolkien dimension was almost a danger. I then went against this, and decided I would enter it at any time I chose, but with this golden rule (with this phial glowing on my desk?) that I must be able to emerge, to shut the book, and get up from the chair. If I can't, I will earn the disapproval of the author. He was an upright man in the real world, and had no intention of casting a spell on anyone. I told him once of a young man who thought he was Frodo. "I've ruined their lives," he said disconsolately.

EPISODE IV brings me up to the present time, and to the new musical addition to the Song Cycle, "Bilbo's Last Song." This came into music instinctively as a solo-plus-chorus; the soloist of the song cycle, joined by a group. What group? The tune exists obviously as a solo melody. But my imagination is curiously full of choral voices, holding Bilbo's story within their harmonies. Yes, the soloist has in my mind slowly become Bilbo himself. It is the end of the Road, and Bilbo now craves companions. He has travelled so long; first cheerfully and jauntily as "Upon the Hearth the Fire Is Red"; then as a tree-herd through the ever-changing seasons; then as Sam Gamgee alone on the mountain passes of Mordor, picking up the dreaded ring and uttering "In Western Lands." As Galadriel and her Elves intone to him their lamenting farewell, Bilbo travels on until eventually he is again by the red hearth, reminiscing. The Elves' voices are at his door. He hears them in his mind, but in performances I began to ask my own group of singers to pick up these "outside" voices for me, while I sang Bilbo's solo. The voices at the door became real for me.

"Errantry" I began to see as Bilbo's long encore. He retells his Odyssey, but the mood has become lighter, more delicate, dare one say, faerier. Tom Bombadil's lyric has the most complex rhyming scheme ever to have been thought up. Bilbo is taxed by this tour de force, and he asks companions to help him out. This strong feeling within me has produced the chorus indications now seen in "Errantry." Though Bilbo is ever present, other voices take individual lines; short passages of harmony enrich the sound here and there, and finally give the song a coda. Bilbo has courted, fought and explored. He arrives at the remotest point, and there on the "little isles that lonely lay" he finds "naught but blowing grass." He realises that with much wandering he has forgotten his message. Bilbo takes a deep pause . . . then starts again "for ever still a messenger, a passenger, a tarrier." "Errantry" was the end of the song cycle, until "Bilbo's Last Song" stood on my music desk.

"Day is ended," now says Bilbo, "Journey long before me lies," (still). "But the sails are set and we are going to islands behind the sun. Rest is in sight." As I read the poem I felt a surge of hope that at last even the weather-driven mariner of the last line of "Errantry" would find a home. The Elves are with him, as they were so often with Frodo, accompanying him and consoling him. Most wonderful of all, after cycles of life-times on earth, the Elves have taken to the sea. "Bilbo's Last Song" is awash with sea metaphors. It was deeply moving to perform this piece at the Commemoration for Michael Flanders who loved the sea more than anything else. Could it be that at the very end Tolkien expressed another profoundly important streak in the English character, the love of the sea? Tolkien, whose name was Viking (he was proud of that), closes Bilbo's story with lines that Vikings and British alike have repeated with infinite variations:

Lands there are to West of West,
Where night is quiet and sleep is rest.

DONALD SWANN

CONTENTS

THE ROAD GOES
EVER ON

MUSICAL NOTES
FOR PERFORMERS

SOLOISTS. The voice range of the song cycle is baritone or mezzo soprano, but the soloist in the last item, "Bilbo's Last Song," is to be supported by mixed voices — up to G — (for composer's reasons, see foreword). However, middle or lower voices wishing to sing "Bilbo's Last Song" as a solo are asked to transpose down.

CHOIRS. I have given indications of voice divisions as from "Namárië" to the end (songs 5.6.7.8). I can imagine this group of the last four songs as a "Tolkien Solo-with-Chorus" contribution to a choral concert; giving the chorus a chance to sing a plainsong chant, to help their soloist out with an Elvish countermelody, to dovetail a fast and tripping lyric, and finally to end with a broad melody.

GUITARISTS. Chord symbols will be found for the songs suitable to their instrument (nos. 1.2.4.6.8). The interlude melodic line can also be picked out by the guitar in song no. 5.

THE ROAD GOES EVER ON

ev - er on and on,   And whith-er then?   I can_ not_ say.

UPON THE HEARTH THE FIRE IS RED

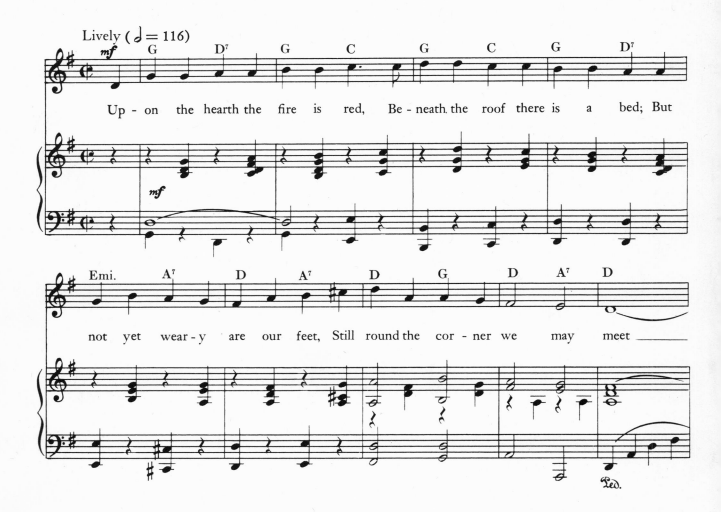

IN THE WILLOW-MEADS OF TASARINAN

light and the mu-sic in the Sum-mer by the Sev-en Riv-ers of Os-sir! And I

thought that was best. To the beech-es of Nel-dor-eth I

came in the Au-tumn. Ah! the gold and the red and the sigh-ing of leaves in the

Au - tumn in Taur - na - nel - dor! It was more than my de - sire.

To the pine - trees up - on the high - land of Dor - tho - nion I climbed in the

Win - ter. Ah! the wind and the white-ness and the black branch-es of

14

ro - na, in Tau - re - mor - na, in Ald - a -

ló - më, In my own land, in the coun - try of Fan - gorn,

Where the roots are long, And the years lie thick - er than the leaves In

Tau - re - mor - na - ló - - - më.

IN WESTERN LANDS

deep, be-yond all tow-ers strong and high, be-yond all moun-tains

steep, a-bove all shad-ows rides the Sun and Stars for ev-er

dwell: I will not say the Day is done, nor bid the Stars fare-

21

NAMÁRIË (FAREWELL)

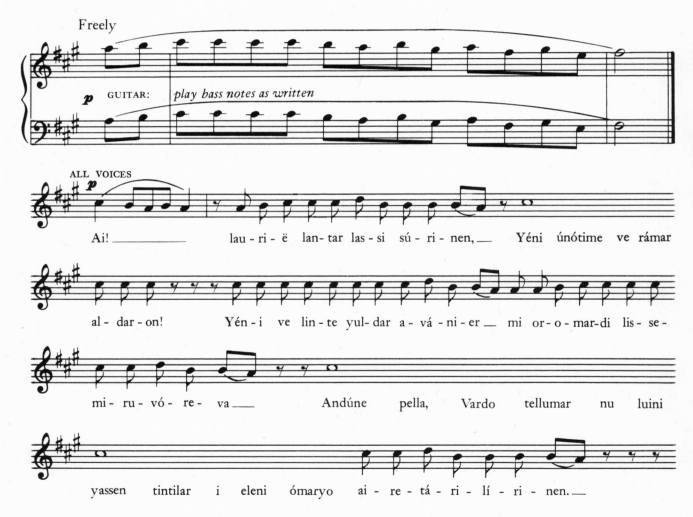

Note: Division of voices in last four songs of cycle: the instructions apply when performed with a choir. Otherwise a solo singer should sing the top line in all *divisi* passages. For the translation of the Elvish text see pages 66–67.

Sí man i yulma nin en-quan-tu-va? __

p GUITAR *as before*

poco rit.

SOLO
a tempo primo

An sí Tintalle Varda Oi - o - los - së - o ve fan - yar máryat Elentári or - ta - ne

ALL

SOLO
cresc. poco a poco

ar il - ye ti - er un - du - lá - ve lum - bu - le; __ ar sindanóriello

23

caita mornië i falmalinnar imbe met, ar hísië untúpa Cala - cir - yo

mí - ri oi - a - le.___ Sí van - wa ná, Ró - mel - lo van - wa, Va - li - mar!___

Na - má - ri - ë! ___ Nai hi hi - ru - valyë Va - li - mar.

Nai el - yë hi - ru - va.___ Na - má - ri - ë! ___

I SIT BESIDE
THE FIRE

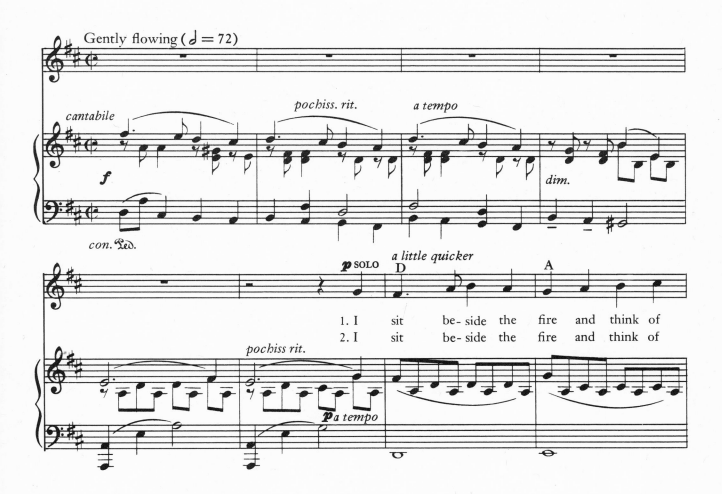

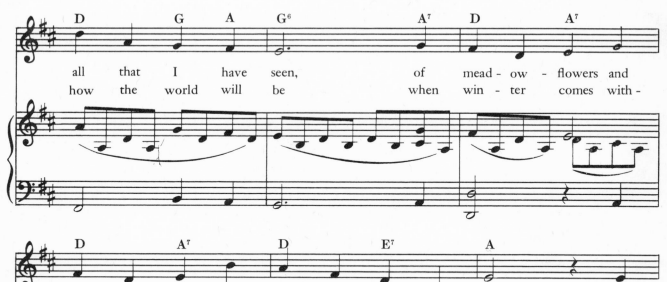

all that I have seen, of mead-ow-flowers and
how the world will be when win-ter comes with-

but-ter-flies in sum-mers that have been; Of
out a spring that I shall ev-er see. For

yel-low leaves and gos-sa-mer in au-tumns that there were, with
still there are so man-y things that I have nev-er seen: in

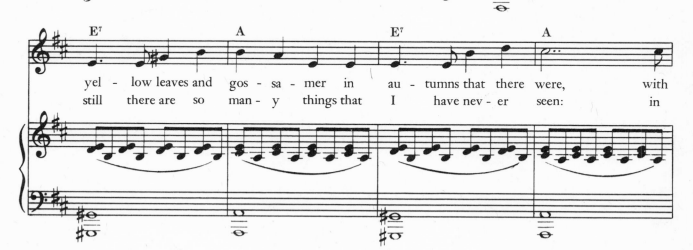

D.C. for Verse 2

morn - ing mist and sil - ver sun and wind up - on my hair. __
ev - ery wood in ev - ery spring there is a differ - ent green. __

tempo primo

cantabile   pochiss rit.   a tempo

con Ped.

A⁷ *pp*   D *a little quicker*   A

3. I   sit be - side the fire and think of

pochiss rit.   a tempo

a little quicker

peo-ple long a - go, and peo-ple who will see a world that

I shall nev - er know. But all the while I sit and think of

times there were be - fore, I lis - ten for re - turn - ing feet and

Note: For the translation of the Elvish text see pages 66–67.

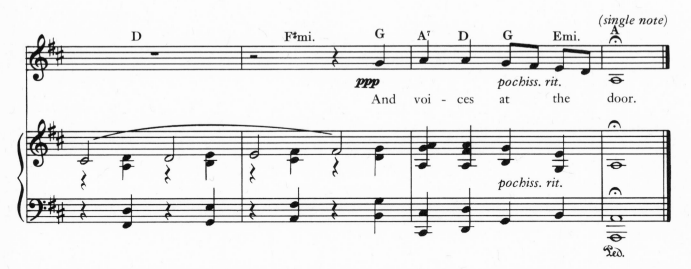

And voi - ces at the door.

(single note)

ppp   *pochiss. rit.*

pochiss. rit.

Ped.

Note: This song may be connected with Number 7 by sustaining the pedal at the end of Number 6 and moving directly on to Number 7.

ERRANTRY

Note: Division of voices: some may prefer to use soloists, or two men or two girls, for many entries. My indications are obviously for the choirmaster's discretion.

There
was a mer-ry pas-sen-ger, a mes-sen-ger, a mar-i-ner: he
built a gild-ed gon-do-la to wan-der in, and had in her a

33

load of yel-low o-ran-ges and por-ridge for his prov-en-der; he

per-fumed her with mar-jo-ram and car-da-mom and la-ven-der.

landed all in lone - li - ness where ston - i - ly the peb - bles on the

run - ning riv - er Der - ri - lyn go mer - ri - ly for ev - er on.

He jour - neyed then through mead - ow - lands to

Shad-ow-land that drear-y lay, and un-der hill and o-ver hill went

rov-ing still a wear-y way. He sat and sang a

mel-o-dy, his er-rant-ry a-tar-ry-ing; he

begged a pret-ty but-ter-fly that flut-tered by to mar-ry him. She

scorned him and she scoffed at him, she laughed at him un-

pit-y-ing; so long he stud-ied wiz-ard-ry and sig-ald-ry and

feath - er wing of swal - low - hair. He caught her in be - wil - der - ment with

fil - a - ment of spi - der - thread; he made her soft pa -

vil - i - ons of lil - ies, and a brid - al bed of

40

flow-ers and of this-tle-down to nes-tle down and rest her in; and

silk-en webs of film-y white and sil-ver light he dressed her in.

BASSES *p*

He thread-ed gems in neck-la-ces, but reck-less-ly she squan-dered them and

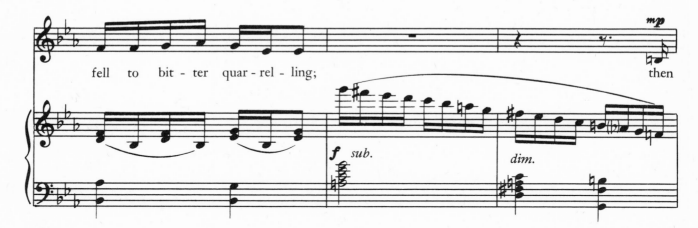

fell to bit-ter quar-rel-ling; then

sor-row-ing he wan-dered on, and there he left her with-er-ing, as

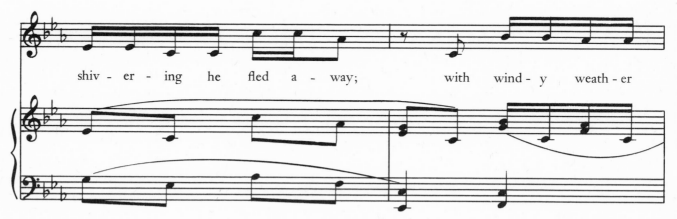

shiv-er-ing he fled a-way; with wind-y weath-er

fol - low - ing on swal - low - wing he sped a - way. He

passed the ar - chi - pel - a - goes where yel - low grows the mar - i - gold, where

count - less sil - ver foun - tains are, and moun - tains are of fair - y - gold. He

took to war and for - ay - ing, a - har - ry - ing be - yond the sea, and

roam - ing o - ver Bel - ma - rie and Thel - la - mie and Fan - ta - sie.

SOPRANOS
pp but forcefully

He made a shield and mo - ri - on of

riding by and chal-lenged him. Of crys-tal was his hab-er-geon, his

scab-bard of chal-ced-o-ny; with sil-ver tipped at ple-ni-lune his

spear was hewn of eb-on-y. His jave-lins were of mal-a-chite and

sta - lac - tite he bran - dished them, and went and fought the drag - on - flies of

Par - a - dise, and van - quished them.

He

bat - tled with the Dum - ble - dors, the Hum - mer - horns, and Hon - ey - bees,

Altos:mm

and so at last the on-ly way he
took, and turned, and com-ing home with hon-ey-comb, to mem-o-ry his
mes-sage came, and er-rand too!
In derring-do
and glamoury
he had forgot them,
journeying and tourneying,
a wanderer.

a weath-er-driv-en mar-i-ner.

BILBO'S LAST SONG

(AT THE GREY HAVENS)

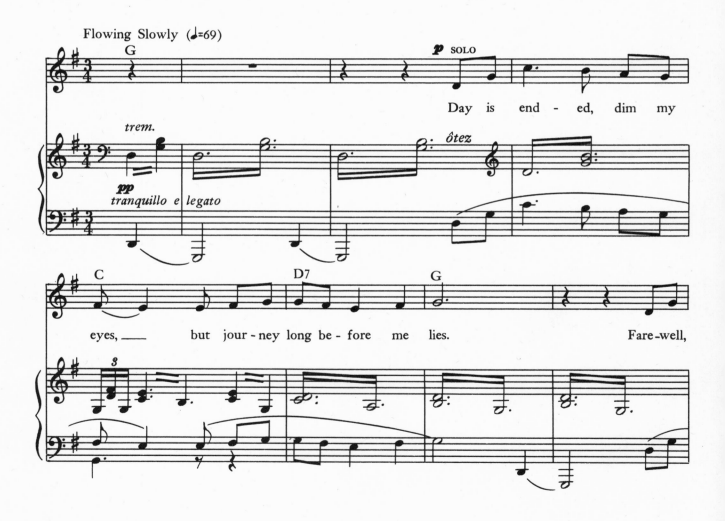

hear the ris - ing of the Sea.

Farewell, friends! The sails are set, the wind is east, the moorings fret. Shadows long before me lie, beneath the ever-bending sky, But islands

lie be-hind the sun that I shall raise ere all is done;

Lands there are to west of West, where night is

quiet ___ and sleep is rest. Guid-ed by the Lone-ly

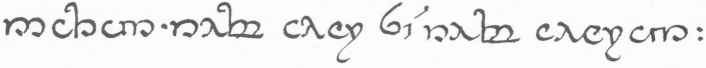

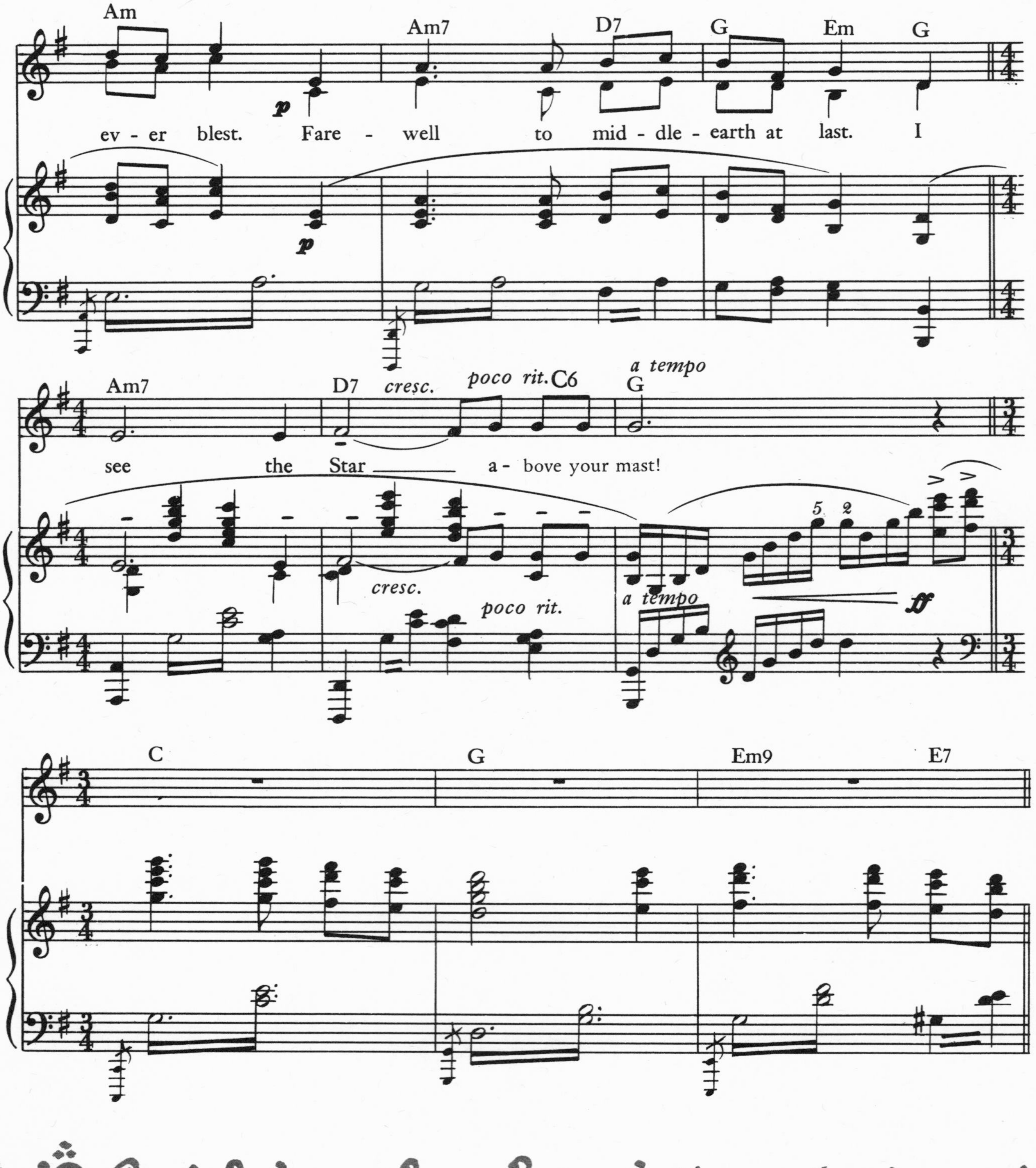
Am
Am7
D7
G
Em
G
ev - er blest. Fare - well to mid - dle - earth at last. I
p
Am7
D7 cresc.
poco rit. C6
a tempo
G
see the Star a - bove your mast!
cresc.
poco rit.
a tempo
ff
C
G
Em9
E7

NOTES AND TRANSLATIONS

Here follow Professor Tolkien's scripts, translations and comments on the Elvish texts for "Namárië" (song Number 5) and "A Elbereth Gilthoniel" (in song Number 6).

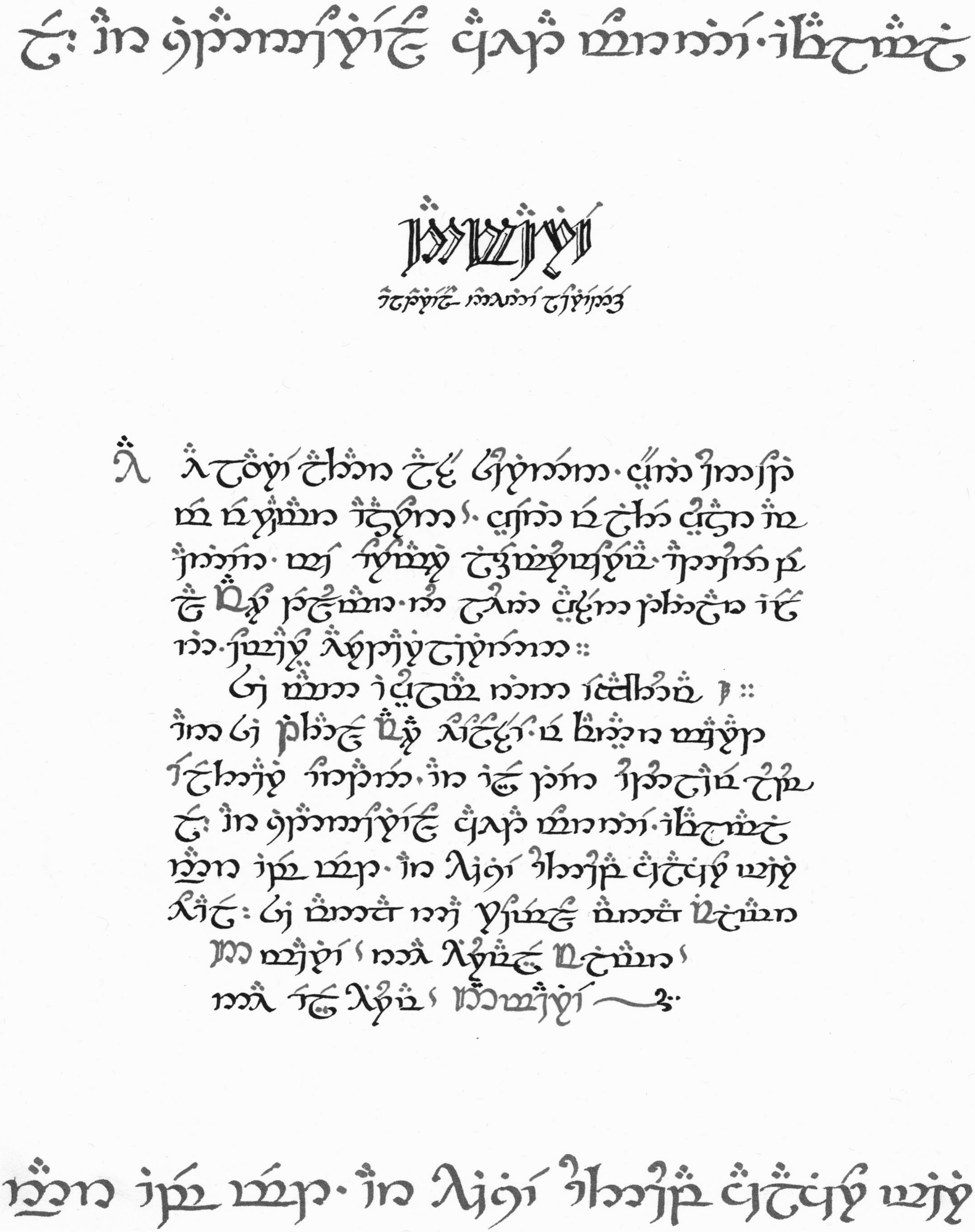

[Tengwar script line]

NAMÁRIË

Altariello nainië Lóriendesse
(Galadriel's lament in Lórien)

The Farewell in *The Lord of the Rings*, Vol. I, p. 394.

1 Ai! láurië lántar lássi súrinèn,
2 yéni ùnótìmè ve rámar áldaròn!
3 Yéni ve línte yúldar avánièr
4 mī óromárdi lísse-mìruvórevà
5 Àndúne pélla Várdo téllumàr
6 nu luíni, yássen tíntilàr i élenì
7 òmáryo aíre-tári-lírinèn.
8 Sì mán i yúlma nín ènquántuvà?
9 An sí Tìntálle Várda Óiolóssëò
10 ve fányar máryat Élentári órtanè,
11 ar ílye tíër ùndu-láve lúmbulè;
12 ar sínda-nórié-llo caíta mórnië
13 i fálmalínnar ímbe mèt, ar hísiè
14 ùn-túpa Càlacíryo míri óialè.
15 Sì vánwa nà, Ròméllo vánwa, Válimàr!
16 Namárië! Nai híruválye Válimàr.
17 Nai élye híruvà. Namárië!

The word-order and style of the chant is "poetic," and it makes concessions to metre. In a clearer and more normal style the words would be arranged as below. Compounded words are indicated by hyphens. A literal translation is written below from which it may be seen that the version given in Vol. I, p. 394 (and here following later) is sufficiently accurate.*

* The text is that of the revised form in the Second Edition, in which a few minor errors of punctuation and quantity marks have been corrected, and *vánier*, line 3, given the more correct (perfect) form *avánier*.

It is assumed that final *e* will be recognised always as a pronounced syllable; and *ë* has only been used to indicate that *ië, ëa, ëo* are dissyllabic. *Long* vowels are marked with a macron ¯, to distinguish this from ´, here used to indicate *major stresses*, usually with rising tone, and ` for *minor stresses*, usually with falling tone.

Words in square brackets are not expressed in the Elvish text.

Ai! lassi   lantar   laurië   sūrinen,   yēni
Alas! leaves   fall (*pl.*)   golden (*pl.*)   wind-in   years (long Elvish years)

ū-nōt-ime   ve aldaron rāmar. Yēni avānier   ve
not-count-able   as   trees-of wings.   Years   have passed away (*pl.*)   like

linte   yuldar   lisse-miruvōre-va mī   oro-mardi
swift (*pl.*)   draughts   sweet-nectar-of   in the   high-halls

Andūne   pella   Vardo   nu luini   tellumar,   yassen
West   beyond (the borders of)   Varda's   under blue   domes,   which-in (*pl.*)

[Tengwar script line]

66

mä ᵗᶜᵍ ⁿⁿᵈ ⁿⁿⁿⁿⁿ

tintilar i eleni ōma-ryo līrinen aire-tārio.
twinkle the stars voice-hers song-in holy-queen's.

Sī man i yulma nin en-quant-uva?
Now who the cup me-for re-fill-will?

An sī Varda, Tintalle, Elen-tāri ortane mā-rya-t
For now Varda, Star-kindler, Star-queen lifted up hands-her-two

Oio-lossëo ve fanyar, ar lumbule undu-
Ever-white-from like (white) clouds and (heavy) shadow down-

-lāve ilye tiër; ar sinda-nōrie-llo mornië
licked all (pl.) roads; and grey-country-from darkness

caita i falma-li-nnar imbe met
lies the foaming waves-many-upon (pl.) between us-two [Varda and Galadriel]

ar hīsië un-tūpa Calaciryo mīri oiale. Sī
and mist down-roofs Kalakirya's jewels everlastingly. Now

vanwa nā, Rōmello vanwa, Valimar.
lost is, [to one] from the East lost, Valimar.

Namārië! Nai hir-uva-lye Valimar.
Farewell! be it that find wilt-thou Valimar.

Nai elye hir-uva. Namārië!
Be it that even thou find will [it] Farewell!

NAMÁRIË

(English translation of the Elvish text in Number 5)

"Ah! like gold fall the leaves in the wind, long years numberless as the wings of trees! The long years have passed like swift draughts of the sweet mead in lofty halls beyond the West, beneath the blue vaults of Varda wherein the stars tremble in the song of her voice, holy and queenly. Who now shall refill the cup for me? For now the Kindler, Varda, the Queen of the Stars, from Mount Everwhite has uplifted her hands like clouds, and all paths are drowned deep in shadow; and out of a grey country darkness lies on the foaming waves between us, and mist covers the jewels of Calacirya for ever. Now lost, lost to those from the East is Valimar! Farewell! Maybe thou shalt find Valimar. Maybe even thou shalt find it. Farewell!"

With regard to the translation above, note that *ortane* (line 10) is rendered "has uplifted." But *ortane* is a past tense and refers to events in the far past. The *sí* (now) in this line is anticipated, and refers to the still enduring present results, described in the present tenses in lines 12–15. This is a Quenya method of saying what would be expressed in E. by: *now, V. having lifted up her hands . . . darkness lies upon the sea between us.*

After the destruction of the Two Trees, and the flight from *Valinor* of the revolting *Eldar*, *Varda* lifted up her hands, in obedience to the decree of *Manwe*, and summoned up the dark shadows which engulfed the shores and the mountains and last of all the *fana* (figure) of Varda, with her hands turned eastward in rejection, standing white upon *Oiolosse*.

The question *Sí man i yulma nin enquantuva?* and the question at the end of her song (Vol. I, p. 389), *What ship would bear me ever back across so wide a Sea?*, refer to the special position of Galadriel. She was the last survivor of the princes and queens who had led the revolting *Noldor* to exile in Middle-earth. After the overthrow of *Morgoth* at the end of the First Age a ban was set upon her return, and she had replied proudly that she had no wish to do so. She passed over the Mountains of *Eredluin* with her husband *Celeborn* (one of the *Sindar*) and went to *Eregion*. But it was impossible for one of the High-Elves to overcome the yearning for the Sea, and the longing to pass over it again to the land of their former bliss. She was now burdened with this desire. In the event, after the fall of *Sauron*, in reward for all that she had done to oppose him, but above all for her rejection of the Ring when it came within her power, the ban was lifted, and she returned over the Sea, as is told at the end of *The Lord of the Rings*.

The last lines of the chant express a wish (or hope) that though she could not go, Frodo might perhaps be allowed to do so. *Nā-i > nai*, "be it that," expresses rather a wish than a hope, and would be more closely rendered "may it be that" (thou wilt find), than by "maybe."

The metre is iambic, in lines of 5 or 6 feet each. The first part, lines 1–7, is in alternating lines: 5, 6, 5, 6, etc. The separate line 8 has also 5 feet. The second part has only lines of 6 feet. As occasional variations on the iamb, lines 2 and 3 begin with a trochee (*yĕni*), and an anapæst occurs in the second foot of line 1, and the fourth of line 3.

The stresses employed metrically were those used in the normal pronunciation of Quenya. The main (high-toned) stress was originally on the first syllable of all words, but in words of 3 or more syllables it had been moved forward to fall on the penultimate syllable, if that was *long;* if it was short, then the main stress fell on the antepenult irrespective of length (as in *éleni*).* The initial syllable usually retained some degree of stress. In long words, especially recognized compounds, it was, though lower in tone, often equal in force to the main stress: as in *óromárdi*,

* Long syllables were those containing a long vowel, a dipththong (as *au, ai, oi, ui*), or a vowel followed by two consonants.

fálmalínnar, etc. It was weaker when immediately preceding the main stress, as in *Àndúne*, *òmáryo*, *Tìntálle*, *Ròméllo*; and in such cases, if it was short it became unstressed, as in *avániër*. (Compare E. *almighty*, *ècónomy*, *éconómical*.) The weaker stresses can be employed as the metrical stresses, or in the place of unstressed elements, according to their position. They are used as unstressed syllables only when immediately followed by a main stress as in *Andúne*, etc.

Final vowels were normally short and unstressed, in words of more than one syllable, if they followed the main stress, as in *lassi*, *linte*, *yulma*, etc. But they had nearly all formerly been long vowels (or they would have disappeared), so that in the very frequent cases of words ending in two short syllables, as *ūnótime*, *tellumar*, *lumbule*, *hīsië*, etc., they received a light stress that could be used metrically. This is seen especially at the ends of lines, which in a highly inflected language like Quenya will naturally have as a final word one ending in inflexions or derivative suffixes. In fact, in this chant all the lines end in this way, except 15 and 16, which end in the compound *Vali-mar* ("dwelling of the Valar"). A similar use of an inflexional ending within the line is seen only in lines 6, 17: *tīntilàr*, *híruvà*. In exclamatory words such as *namārië*, the length of the final vowel was often retained, and could in a farewell cry be much extended.

When myself reciting this chant, I usually begin it with an extra-metrical and extended version of *ai!* ("alas!"): āáāāī, and then repeat *ai* within the metre.

miruvóre. According to the Eldar, a word derived from the language of the Valar; the name that they gave to the drink poured out at their festivals. Its making and the meaning of its name were not known for certain, but the Eldar believed it to be made from the honey of the undying flowers in the gardens of Yavanna, though it was clear and translucent. [Compare the νέκταρ of the Olympian gods. But the connexion of this word with "honey" is mainly due to modern botanists (though Euripides used νέκταρ μελισσᾶν, "divine drink of bees," as a poetic periphrasis for "honey"). A probable etymological meaning of νέκταρ is "death-defeater." Cf. αμβροσία "immortality," the food of the gods.]

Tintalle. "She that causes sparkling, kindles lights." For *tin-*, cf. *tintilar*, "sparkle, glitter." The Q. *tinwe*, "spark," was, like S. *gil* (see the notes on the chant "A Elbereth"), often used in sense of "star."

Varda. "The Exalted," greatest of the queens of the *Valar*, spouse of the "Elder King" (*Manwe*, the Lord of the Valar). The S. name *Elbereth* means "Star-queen."

Oiolosse. Another, and later more usual, name for *Tániquetil* ("high white peak"), the highest of the *Pelóri*, the Mountains of Valinor, and so of all mountains then on earth. Upon its summit were the domed halls* of *Manwe* and *Varda*. The element *oi*, *oio* meant "ever, everlastingly." Cf. *oiale*. The stem *los* was applied to fallen snow. The Q. forms were adj. *losse*, "snow-white," and n. *losse*, "fallen snow"; the S. forms

---

* *Oromardi*, *tellumar*.

loss, "snow" [cf. the *Lossoth* (*loss-hoth*), the Snowmen. Appendix A, Vol. III, pp. 321–22]; *lossen*, "snowy," and an adj. *glos(s)*, "dazzling-white," with an augmentative *g*- in S. often prefixed to *l*-. *Oiolosse* thus meant "Ever-snow-white." The S. form was *Uilos;* see note on *Fanuilos* under Sam's invocation.

Calaciryo. Gen. of *Cala-cirya*, "light-cleft," the great ravine in the mountains of Valinor, through which the light of the Blessed Realm, coming from the Two Trees, flowed out into the long shorelands of Valinor, east of the mountains. There most of the Eldar had formerly dwelt, or upon *Eressëa*, "the lonely isle" that lay not far from the shores. On p. 248, Vol. I, appears *Cala-cirian*, anglicized from *Kalakiryan(de)*, the region of *Eldamar* (Elvenhome) in and near the entrance to the ravine, where the Light was brighter and the land more beautiful.

Valimar (also *Valmar*). Properly the city of the Valar, near the mound upon which the Two Trees stood, but it is here used (it means "dwelling of the Valar") to stand for the land of the Valar as a whole, usually called *Valinor*, *Valinóre*.

laure. Translated "gold," but it was not a metallic word. It was applied to those things which we often call "golden" though they do not much resemble metallic gold: golden light, especially sunlight. The derived adj. was *laurëa* (pl. *laurië*), "golden." The reference is to autumn as in Middle-earth (called *lasselanta*, "leaf-fall"), when the yellow leaves released by a wind may fall, fluttering, gleaming in the sun.

(Tengwar inscription)

A ELBERETH GILTHONIEL

The Chant in *The Lord of the Rings*, Vol. I, p. 250.

A Elbereth Gilthoniel,
silivren penna míriel
o menel aglar elenath!
Na-chaered palan-díriel
o galadhremmin ennorath,
Fanuilos, le linnathon
nef aear, sí nef aearon!

This is the opening verse of a chant or hymn, addressed to Varda/Elbereth, evidently similar to that heard by the hobbits in the Shire (Vol. I, pp. 88–89). This verse is, however, reported in the Sindarin, or Grey-elven tongue. It is in accentual iambic metre, each line having 4 feet, arranged in a 7-line stanza, rhyming *aa, b, a, b, cc.*

The intended pronunciation is given in Appendix E to Vol. III but not perhaps with great clarity, so I offer a few notes.

Vowels. Short unless marked ´. Of the long vowels only *í* (as in English *see*) by chance occurs. The short vowels may be rendered as in E. *sick, bed, hot, foot* (for *ŭ*), though *ŏ* is intended to be rounder than in modern E. Short *ă* should *not* have the modern E. sound [æ] as in *cat*, but the same sound (shortened) as in *ah;* both vowels in *aglar*, for instance, should be the same. Of the "long diphthongs" *ae, oe, au, ui*, only *ae* and *ui* appear. The first is meant to represent a sound very similar to the E. [ai] diphthong in *high, lie*, etc.; the second a sound like *ui* in *pursuing* but normally pronounced in one syllable.*

Consonants. C and *g* are both hard (as *k*, and *g* in *give*) in all positions. *Ch* represents the sound spelt *ch* in Welsh, German, Gaelic, and in Russian X. *Ng* represents the same sounds as E. *ng;* that in *sing* finally and initially as in *nguruthos* (Vol. II, p. 339); otherwise as in *finger. Th* is the voiceless E. *th* in *thin growth; dh* the voiced E. *th* in *this weather. F* finally (as in *nef*) is used for *v* (as in E. *of*). Otherwise it is as E. normal *f. R* is a trilled *r*, never silent.

Stress. This is placed as in Quenya (Galadriel's lament): on the first syllable of words of one or two syllables; in longer words on the penult, unless that is *short*, in which case it is placed on the third syllable from the end, as in *El*bereth, Gilth*oni*el, *en*norath, *lin*nathon, etc. All consonants written double are meant to be so pronounced, and so make the syllable long. But consonants represented by *h* added as a "spirantal" sign (*ch, th, ph, dh*) are normally single sounds.

* The first vowel (*a* and *u*) was in both somewhat prolonged. These diphthongs were thus of a length more or less equal to the time occupied by two syllables, and are therefore occasionally employed metrically where the normal metre requires two. *Fanuilos* is an example both on p. 250, Vol. I, and in Sam's invocation, Vol. II, p. 339.

*

(Tengwar inscription)

A ELBERETH GILTHONIEL

A Elbereth	*Gil-thoniel,*	*silivren*		*penna*
O Elbereth	Star-kindler,	(white) glittering		slants-down

míriel		*o*	*menel*	*aglar*	*elenath!*
sparkling like jewels		from	firmament	glory	[of] the star-host

Na-chaered	*palan-*	*-díriel*	*o*
to-remote distance	after-having-	gazed	from

galadh-remmin	*en-nor-ath,*	*Fanuilos,*	*le*	*linnathon*
tree-tangled	middle-lands,	Fanuilos,	to thee	I will chant

nef	*aear*	*sí*	*nef*	*aearon.*
on this side of	ocean	here	on this side of	the Great Ocean.

Compare Sam's invocation in Vol. II, p. 339:

*A Elbereth Gilthoniel o menel palan-diriel,**	*le*	*nallon*
	gazing afar	to thee	I cry

sí	*di-nguruthos!*	*A*	*tiro**	*nin, Fanuilos!*
here	beneath-death-horror.		look towards (watch over)	me, Fanuilos!

O! ELBERETH

(English translation of the Elvish text occurring in "I Sit beside the Fire")

O! Elbereth who lit the stars, from glittering crystal slanting falls with light like jewels from heaven on high the glory of the starry host. To lands remote I have looked afar, and now to thee, Fanuilos, bright spirit clothed in ever-white, I here will sing beyond the Sea, beyond the wide and sundering Sea.
O! Queen who kindled star on star, white-robed from heaven gazing far, here overwhelmed in dread of Death I cry: O guard me, Elbereth!

The language is Sindarin, but of a variety used by the High Elves (of which kind were most of the Elves in Rivendell), marked in high style and verse by the influence of Quenya, which had been originally their normal tongue. Examples of this are: *menel*, "firmament, high heaven, the region of the stars"*; *palan-*, "afar," more accu-

* By an error which has escaped my attention in various corrections the *i* in these words is marked *í* (as long). It should be short.

* Not thought of by the Elves as a "firmament" or fixed sphere. The word was a Q. invention from *men* (direction, region) + *el* (the basis of many star-words).

rately "abroad, far and wide"; *le*, the reverential 2nd person sing. Complete translation representing the full meaning and associations of the words would be more lengthy. For instance, *silivren* would recall to Elvish minds the *silmarils* and describe the stars as crystalline forms shining from within with a light of mysterious power.* *Fanuilos* is also a name of full meaning; see below.

I do not attempt to analyse the language or exhibit its relation to Quenya. But the kinship of the two languages can be observed, even in these fragments.

1. The ancient element EL, "star," in Q. *elen* (pl. *eleni*), S. *êl* (pls. *elin*, *elenath*) in *Elbereth*, *elenath*. In S. this was in ordinary language largely replaced by *gil*, "bright spark," as in *Gilthoniel*, *Gil-galad*, "Star of bright light," *Os(t)giliath*, "Fortress of the Stars."
2. The stem *mîr*, "jewel," as in the Lament and in *míriel*.
3. The word *aglar*, "glory," is of the same origin as Q. *alcar*, "glory"; cf. *alcarin*, "glorious," as title of King *Atanamir*.
4. *galadh* is same word in S. form as Q. *alda*, "tree" (*aldaron*, "of trees," in the Lament).
5. *aear*, "Sea," is in Q. *ëar* (as in *Earendil*, etc.); *aearon* has an augmenting suffix.
6. The stem TIR, "to look at (towards), watch, watch over," occurs in Q. *palantír* and in *Tirion*, "great watch-tower," Vol. I, pp. 247, 389, Vol. II, p. 204; in S. *palandíriel*, *-díriel* [with S. change

* Both *silivren* and *silma-ril* contain the name *Silima* that Feanor gave to the crystal substance he devised and alone could make.

of medial *t* > *d*], and in *tiro* (imperative) in Sam's invocation.

As a "divine" or "angelic" person *Varda/ Elbereth* could be said to be "looking afar from heaven" (as in Sam's invocation); hence the use of a present participle.* She was often thought of, or depicted, as standing on a great height looking towards Middle-earth, with eyes that penetrated the shadows, and listening to the cries for aid of Elves (and Men) in peril or grief. Frodo (Vol. I, p. 208) and Sam both invoke her in moments of extreme peril. The Elves sing hymns to her. (These and other references to religion in *The Lord of the Rings* are frequently overlooked.)

The Elves in Rivendell could only be said to "gaze afar" in yearning. But actually the form used in the hymn is *palandíriel* (past part.), "having gazed afar." This is a reference to the *palantír* upon the Tower Hills (the "Stone of Elendil"); see note 2 in Appendix A, Vol. III, p. 322. This alone of the *palantíri* was so made as to look out only west over the Sea. After the fall of Elendil the High-Elves took back this Stone into their own care, and it was not destroyed, nor again used by Men.

The High-Elves (such as did not dwell in or near the Havens) journeyed to the Tower Hills at intervals to look afar at *Eressëa* (the Elvish isle) and the Shores of Valinor, close to which it lay. The hymn in Vol. I, p. 250, is one appropriate to Elves who have just returned from such a pilgrimage.

No doubt Gildor and his companions (Vol. I.,

* With short *dir*.

Chap. 3), since they appear to have been going eastward, were Elves living in or near Rivendell returning from the *palantír* of the Tower Hills. On such visits they were sometimes rewarded by a vision, clear but remote, of Elbereth, as a majestic figure, shining white, standing upon the mountain *Oiolosse* (S. *Uilos*). It was then that she was also addressed by the title *Fanuilos*.

Elbereth was the usual name in S. of the *Vala*, called in Q. *Varda*, "the Exalted." It is more or less the equivalent of Q. *Elentári*, "Star-queen" (Vol. I, p. 394); but *bereth* actually meant "spouse," and was used of one who is "queen" as spouse of a king.* *Varda* was spouse of Manwe, "the Elder King," chief of the Valar.

Fanuilos. The title of Elbereth (see above), which is rendered "Snow-white" (Vol. I, p. 88), though this is very inadequate. *Fana-* is an Elvish element, with primary meaning "veil." The S. form *fân*, *fan-* was usually applied to clouds, floating as veils over the blue sky or the sun or moon, or resting on hills.†

In Quenya, however, the simple word *fana* acquired a special sense. Owing to the close association of the High-Elves with the *Valar*, it was applied to the "veils" or "raiment" in which the *Valar* presented themselves to physical eyes. These were the bodies in which they were self-incarnated. They usually took the shape of the bodies of Elves (and Men). The *Valar* assumed these forms when, after their demiurgic labours, they came and dwelt in *Arda*, "the Realm." They did so because of their love and desire for the Children of God (*Erusēn*), for whom they were to prepare the "realm." The future forms of Elves and Men had been revealed to them, though they had no part in their design or making, and the precise time of their appearance was not known. In these *fanar* they later presented themselves to the Elves,* and appeared as persons of majestic (but not gigantic) stature, vested in robes expressing their individual natures and functions. The High-Elves said that these forms were always in some degree radiant, as if suffused with a light from within. In Quenya, *fana* thus came to signify the radiant and majestic figure of one of the great *Valar*.† In Sindarin, especially as used by the High-Elves, the originally identical word *fân* (*fan-*), "cloud," was also given the same sense. *Fan-uilos* thus in full signified "bright (angelic) figure ever white (as snow)."

I have often had questions about the grammatical features appearing in the Sindarin fragments. There is no time for answering these. But I might mention the ending -*ath*. In S. plurals were mostly made with vowel-changes: *Adan*, *Edain*; *orch*, *yrch*; etc. But the suffix -*ath* (originally a collective noun-suffix) was used as a group plural, embracing all things of the same name, or those associated in some special arrange-

* Cf. E. *queen:* originally an ancient word for wife or woman, already in Old English usually reserved for the king's wife. (But not so in any of the related languages.)

† Cf. the adj. *fanui*, "cloudy" (with -*ui* as in *lithui*, "ashy," in *Ered Lithui*), appearing in *Fanui-dhol*, "Cloudyhead," a mountain-name (Vol. I, p. 296, etc.).

* Though they could also assume other wholly "inhuman" shapes, which were seldom seen by Elves or Men.

† In the sense of "cloud," in Quenya the derivative *fanya* was used, as in Galadriel's lament.

ment or organization. So *elenath* (as plural of *êl*, pl. *elin*) meant "the host of the stars": sc. (all) the (visible) stars of the firmament. Cf. *ennorath*, the group of central lands, making up Middle-earth. Note also *Argonath*, "the pair of royal stones," at the entrance to Gondor; *Periannath*, "the Hobbits (as a race)," as collective pl. of *perian*, "halfling" (pl. *periain*). The *ath* is not a genitive inflexion as some have guessed. In S. the simple genitive was usually expressed by placing the genitival noun in adjectival position (in S. *after* the primary noun). So Vol. I, p. 319, *Ennyn Durin Aran Moria*, "doors (of) Durin King (of) Moria"; Vol. III, p. 41, *Ernil i Pheriannath*, "Prince (of) the Halflings"; Vol. I, p. 320, *Fennas nogothrim*, "gateway (of) dwarf-folk."

*

Professor Tolkien's original manuscript for the English transliteration of Namárië appears on the following page.

Namárië

'farewell'

Altariello nainie Lóriendesse
'Galadriel's lament in Lórien'.

1 Ai! laurië lantar lassi súrinen, |
2 yéni | únótime ve rámar aldaròn! |||
3 Yéni ve lìnte yuldar avánier
4 mì óromardi lisse-miruvóreva ||
5 Andúne pella Vardo tellumar
6 nu luini, yassen tintilar | i eleni
7 ómaryo aire-tári-lírinen. |||

8 Sì man | i yulma nin enquantuva ? |||

9 An sí | Tintalle Varda Oiolosseò |
10 ve fanyar máryat Elentári ortane, ||
11 ar ilye tier undu-lave lumbule; ||
12 ar sinda-nóriè-llo caita mórnie
13 i falmalinnar imbe mèt, || ar hísie
14 un-túpa Calaciryo mìri oiale. ||
15 Sì vanwa nä | Rómello vanwa, Valimàr! |||

16 Namárie ! ||| Nai hiruvalye Valimàr. ||
17 Nai elye hiruva. || Namárie ! |||

The text is that of the revised form in the Second Edition, in which a few minor errors of punctuation and quantity marks have been corrected, and vánier , line 3, given the more correct (perfect) form avánier.

It is assumed that final e will be recognized always as a pronounced syllable ; and ë has only been used to indicate that ie , ëo are disyllabic. Long vowels are marked with macron —, to distinguish this from ' here used to indicate major stresses, usually with rising tone , and ` above minor stress, usually with falling tone. The marks | || ||| indicate the pauses in the chant in ascending order of time-length and tone-fall.